MW00780303

The Goddess You
Principles forLiving in Soul Alignment
Intuitive Journal
By Jeanne Street.

Published by: Inspirit by Design, a division of Jeanne Street LLC, New Milford, Connecticut
Cover & interior design and illustrations by: Kari Del Vecchio of Kari D. Designs. Bridgewater, Connecticut

Library of Congress Control Cataloging- in- Publication Data
available on file

ISBN: 978-0-9974666-0-7

First Edition, November 11, 2016
Printed in the United States of America

The Goddess You
Principles for Living in Soul Alignment

Intuitive Journal

By
Jeanne Street

Illustrated By Kari Del Vecchio

INSPIRIT
HEAL   LEARN   GROW
By Design
New Milford CT

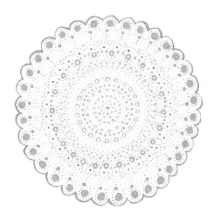

Life is a miracle to cherish and share with others

For
My identical cousin, Kari

Thank you from the depth of my soul for sharing your
beauty, talents and friendship
that has awakened and
energized the spiritual work that
is here to help and guide.

The Goddess You
Interactive Intuitive Journal

Welcome, Goddess You!

This journal is your place to track your personal transformational journey. I am so excited to kick off this adventure with you!

Before we jump in, please look over the following guidelines for implementing your journal practice. They will help you stay focused and obtain your goal of living in soul alignment.

Book plug – you know I just have to – in my book *The Goddess You*: Principles for Living in Soul Alignment, I introduce the 12 main principles for living within. These principles were taught to me by Spirit. They allowed me to obtain my personal soul alignment.

I created this journal as a companion to my book to facilitate a natural flow from one to the other. I recommend that you have both the book *The Goddess You*: Principles for Living in Soul Alignment and your *The Goddess You Journal* in order to follow each lesson fully, with depth and understanding. The guided meditations found throughout *The Goddess You*: Principles for Living in Soul Alignment will also help you get the most out of your work. I will use the 12 principles and guided writing prompts throughout this journal to help you go deeper within. You will be rockin' out your Goddess self in no time!

Follow this link to purchase the book. ***www.jeannestreet.com***

Commitment

I've found the most effective way to stay on track with a new action such as journaling or meditation is to make a commitment to thy self. This commitment will help you remember why you are undertaking this new action—even when it becomes uncomfortable or stagnant. By writing your goals, desires and aspirations down, you energetically align yourself with this new action.

Now, let's be honest: we all get off-track from time to time. That is why it is important to have a contract in place to remind us to stay accountable for this soul work. You are contracting with your soul self to uncover what is keeping you from living in YOUR soul alignment.

Time Frame

Choosing your time frame is also part of your commitment. I offer 12 principles to implement into your life. Each principle is broken into four separate writing prompts. That totals 48 daily journal entries with a couple of bonus prompts for you to go further.

If you work fast and don't tend to need blocks of time to reflect, then you should choose to do this journal in 48 days.

If you like to spend time, hang out for a bit, and let one lesson sink in before rushing into the next lesson, then you should choose the 48-week commitment. If you're a gal who can't seem to make up her mind, I suggest you go for the 48 weeks; you can always move ahead if and when you're ready.

The Goddess You Journal Contract

I_____ am signing this sacred
contract with my soul self. I promise my soul self that I will journal each and every day at
_____o'clock for a minimum of 20 minutes each day. I will forgive myself if I happen to
skip a day as long as I have a very good reason. I will be sure to get back on track as soon as
I am able.   My time frame for this journal and soul work is 48 _days_ or _weeks._ (circle one)
My goals for this journal are:_____

_____

_____

_____

_____

_____

_____

_____

My desired outcome is:_____

_____

_____

_____

_____

_____

_____

_____

Signed_____Date_____

The Un-Rules

Use this journal to expand your thoughts with the guided journal prompts. The best part about this is that there are no rules. You can go in order, if that suits your fancy, or skip around to topics that draw you in. When journaling, it is best not to conform to spelling or grammar rules. If you feel like writing sideways, then do so. Listening to your intuition will lead you to discovering far more than you would if you were worried about conforming to rules. If you have a hard time without following some sort of guideline, then start on the first page and go from there. Again, I urge you to please try to let go of perfectionism as much as you can—this will allow your lovely inner voice to come forward.

Meditation

Use the breathing techniques and meditations in my book *The Goddess You*: Principles for Living in Soul Alignment, to get you in the perfect Zen mode.

You get what you give

What you put in is what you get out. So, my friend, plan accordingly by setting time and space for this sacred work. My advice is to set aside 20 minutes per journaling session. It's best if the sessions take place at the same time of day. This will help you set the framework for using journaling throughout your life as a tool and modality in connecting to your soul self.

Discovering

Let go and have some fun with your writing. The use of colorful pens and pencils can raise the vibration of your writing. Grab a glue stick and use photos and personal items to tell your truths in these pages.

Tissues

Journaling can bring up feelings and thoughts you did not know were even there. It's a grand idea to keep facial tissues on hand. Trust me on this one. I'm speaking from teary-eyed, runny-nosed, sobbing experience here. As I wrote in *The Goddess You*, it was worth every tear, so don't give up on your goals over a few tears. You've got this!

Shhh... Close your lips

Journaling is sacred work; treat it as such. Don't go spilling your deep dark thoughts to others just yet. Right now is the time to let the words loose and release the energy they hold within you. That is key in healing through journaling. Silence is golden, as they say, so spend time listening more and speaking less. This will help you in hearing your soul truths over all the outward noise.

This, my friend, is how you discern what is yours and what is another's.

Writer's block

It happens to the best of us. Yup, I am speaking from experience here, and what I found is that it is best to let go and write anything. Words of gratitude, a prayer, a song, your kid's names, your vows to yourself. I don't care what you write, just that you write through the block! Be silly. Make rhymes. Try writing swear words—it's fun to do in all caps! Do what ever you can to keep your journal commitment!

Ready set GOOOOO

I think you have the idea now! So let's get this party started! I'll see you in the first chapter!

Ohhh, and just one more thing: Remember these are either daily or weekly journal exercises. (Refer back to your contract for your time frame.) If you choose the weekly prompts, then keep in mind you will be journaling on the same prompt for seven days in a row. But feel free to move ahead at your own pace.

Now I'm sending you off with my blessings, prayers and love. May you achieve your goals, and may your journey fill your life with profound love and grace.

Principle
One

Quieting the Mind

It's time to stop the mindless chatter that keeps your brain busy in the nothingness it has to offer. Shutting down the constant chatter will open space for your soul self to be able to emerge forward.

Ego, or as I refer to him, Ego Shmego, is the tricky little bastard that lives in your head and keeps you living in fear. His main job is to generate fear-based thinking and keep it going. He thrives and grows stronger with every fearful thought. The more you turn your attention away from love, the happier and stronger Shmego becomes. By learning how to shift your fear thoughts over to love thoughts, you will begin to recognize Shmego's number. Once you've got his number, you can call him out on the fear he serves up to you and replace that with love. And in case you aren't aware of this truth already, let me tell you what Spirit has taught me about the miracle of love: it is love that heals everything. Bam, now you know the secret universal truth.

I Am Ego Shmego

Breath work keeps your mind free of thoughts that clog your brain's pores, so to speak. Use the guided meditation in chapter one of *The Goddess You* book to prepare your mind, body and soul.

❀ Just a reminder that your daily prompts are the questions your soul self asks. When you respond, you are responding to your Goddess soul self!

❀ "Nancy Drew it" is a coined phrase by moi. When you "Nancy Drew it," you become a detective by uncovering all the hidden details of the question at hand. Nancy Drew is a fictional teenage girl detective invented by author Carolyn Keene in the 1930s book series by the same name.

Let's talk about Ego Shmego and his tone. In *The Goddess You*, I use the word "tone" in a very specific way—it refers to how I hear Spirit's voice. While the dictionary definition of "tone" is simply a modulating of voice that may express a particular feeling or mood, for me the word encompasses the sound or quality through which someone speaks through any one of my senses. Tones can be dull and flat or bright and energetic. Tones can reveal the truth beneath what is happening. Ego Shmego's tone is fear.

Tell me about the words, thoughts and feelings that Shmego uses to keep you living in fear.

2

Groove in LOVE energy for this entry by breathing in through your nose and out through your mouth, while focusing on your heart center for five minutes. Tell me what love sounds and feels like to you right now.

3

Tell me all the things you love about you, and all the ways you love those things. Don't be shy now. Lay all that groovy sexy love on me in the lines below.

4

Now that you are aware of Shmego's tone and love's tone, tell me if and how have you started to call Shmego out on his fear-based tone.

Principle
Two

Self-Love

The golden rule for your life: Forward thinking is love. Backward thinking is fear. You have been mirroring to the world what you think and feel about yourself. This is called the mirror effect. You reflect what you believe about yourself outward, and you receive that energy back in turn. What have you been receiving and how can you change that by shifting your thoughts of you?

Did you know that gratitude opens the heart to receive more love?
Change your attitude with gratitude each and every day and you
will be sure to witness the abundance of love coming your way.

5

Intention convention! Mirror what you feel about yourself and you will receive the love for which you have been longing. Intention rules, so be a wise Goddess You and set your intentions of forward living and thinking below with LOVE.

6

Where In your life have you been denying loves entrance? I am so grateful that you—I mean we—are on this journey. How about you?

_____
_____
_____
_____
_____
_____
_____
_____
_____
_____
_____
_____
_____
_____
_____
_____
_____
_____
_____
_____
_____
_____
_____
_____
_____
_____
_____
_____
_____
_____
_____
_____
_____
_____
_____
_____
_____
_____
_____
_____

7

Choosing love over fear is challenging at times. Tell me all the details of your love / fear challenge. What makes your heart smile today?

8

I believe you are beautiful in every way. Tell me all the truths you believe about this statement. I want all the juicy details!

Principle
Three

Changing your Reactions

Shhh . . . silence is golden, my friend. You can learn a lot about yourself when you quiet your chatter and listen to sounds of life.

I call you, Fairy Godmother Goddess, to grab your wand and pen then repeat after me: If I change my reaction, I change everything.

Sit back now and see the magic appear right before your watchful eyes and quiet lips. You are a remarkable woman who has the power to transform your relationships without roaring your voice!

The real power comes from seeing others with compassion and taking the "I" out of the situation. Get your calm on, and journal until the cows come home—or until you're done, if you don't have cows.

9

Silence truly is golden. It allows you to hear with your heart. Tell me how your heart and eyes can adjust to see others through pure compassion. You can choose to journal about someone who challenges you. But remember Mama's rule: If you don't have anything nice to say, then say nothing at all. Kindness matters. Go to the compassion zone to write.

10

Think before you speak. Tell me how this truth matters to your well-being, and how your attitude has shifted to gratitude.

_____

_____

_____

_____

_____

_____

_____

_____

_____

_____

_____

_____

_____

_____

_____

_____

_____

_____

_____

_____

_____

_____

_____

_____

_____

_____

_____

_____

_____

_____

_____

_____

_____

_____

_____

_____

_____

_____

11

Silence opens up new feelings and views. Share with me how you are embracing these feelings and views and how these changes are felt in your body. Don't be shy with the details. "Nancy Drew it" for me.

12

Share how you have put "changing your reaction" into action. What makes your heart sing with gratitude today?

Principle
Four

Energy Basics

Energy matters, as you read in *The Goddess You*. You are made up of energy, and so are all of your material belongings.

Energy can become stuck and build up, causing energy blocks within your life. Navigating through cobwebs of energy can leave you feeling depleted, like you just need a shower.

These icky, sticky cobwebs of energy can make your day-to-day life a challenge—and cleaning them up is how you discern the difference between your energy and someone else's.

Do a space clearing and watch those webs smudge on out.

13

Let's talk about where the energy is stuck in your life. What does it feel like and look like? How can you help shift it?

_____

_____

_____

_____

_____

_____

_____

_____

_____

_____

_____

_____

_____

_____

_____

_____

_____

_____

_____

_____

_____

_____

_____

_____

_____

_____

_____

_____

_____

_____

_____

_____

_____

_____

_____

_____

_____

_____

_____

_____

14

Letting go of material items can free up space for new energy to come into your life. In what areas can you start to let go of these items? And how can you show gratitude for the items you no longer need?

_____
_____
_____
_____
_____
_____
_____
_____
_____
_____
_____
_____
_____
_____
_____
_____
_____
_____
_____
_____
_____
_____
_____
_____
_____
_____
_____
_____
_____
_____
_____
_____
_____
_____
_____

15

Recognizing the energy is the first step to releasing it. By recognizing the energy, you basically admit to yourself that it is time for change. Change can be challenging until you understand the energy behind it. You can begin to uncover your soul truths by knowing what your feelings are on the release and how your body feels. Tell me all the details of the sensations you notice when you begin to release.

16

Tell me about your energy and how it feels. What color is your energy? Does your energy have shape, taste or form? Put on your detective hat and "Nancy Drew it."

_____
_____
_____

_____
_____
_____
_____
_____
_____
_____
_____
_____
_____
_____
_____
_____
_____
_____
_____
_____
_____
_____
_____
_____
_____
_____
_____
_____
_____
_____
_____
_____
_____
_____

Principle
Five

Healing the Block

The act of forgiveness sets you free from the energy entanglement. True forgiveness, as you have read in *The Goddess You*, comes from your intent to release the block and your faith that you will do so. Forgiveness sets you free from the energy of the block. Sometimes we don't see the need for forgiveness or understand the depth of how the act of forgiving heals the soul. The truth is that when you forgive yourself or someone else, you witness the energy shift; you heal a block that you couldn't even see, due to a false sense or fear-based, backward-living view to which you have been accustomed.

Be sure to use the cycle breathing meditation from chapter one in *The Goddess You* for an open, clear pathway to this soul work you are about to do.

17

Let's talk about why forgiveness matters to your well-being by writing about the things that stop or block you. And by the way, tell me what you are thankful for today.

_____
_____
_____
_____
_____
_____
_____
_____
_____
_____
_____
_____
_____
_____
_____
_____
_____
_____
_____
_____
_____
_____
_____
_____
_____
_____
_____
_____
_____
_____
_____
_____
_____
_____
_____
_____
_____
_____
_____
_____
_____

18

Now that you have the things that block you written down on paper, can you tell me where in your body you feel that block? And be sure to "Nancy Drew it" for me. Give me all the details of how it feels, taste, smells or looks like. Tell me if it has a color or causes pain. Go deep within. Don't be shy. That's why you bought those tissues!

Judgments can hold you hostage. Holding onto what others think about you or what you think of others is sure to clog up your energy like a smelly, dirty sponge. Open your heart center with full compassion. You have been secretly holding onto judgments; tell me about them. That Shmego guy still has some hold on you, and it's time to call him out!

20

Let's talk love and higher power. What does higher power mean to you, and how can you begin to channel that unconditional love into your everyday life?

Principle
Six

Let it Go

Talking about your past can keep you living in a backward view wherein you replay your memories like a Lifetime television series marathon—your life in review, over and over. This action causes you to grow the energy of those stories. As the energy around them grows, the hold these stories have over you builds and builds like a brick wall. The purpose of this wall is to keep you from living forward. The wall becomes larger and larger until you can't see past the bricks. Removing the bricks one by one is your lifeline to aligning to your soul self and restoring your soul truths. Pretty cool, right? Now get ready to tear down that wall.

21

Day one, brick one. Time to tear down the wall. The mortar you used to build the wall will crumble away when you can adjust your view, seeing Shmego as the mortar! Tell me all that you can about this brick wall. Use this journal space for reflections and insights you learned during your clearing ceremony.

22

As you read in *The Goddess You*, a false sense of identity can keep you hostage. Can you see past the wall to your true identity?

_____
_____
_____
_____
_____
_____
_____
_____
_____
_____
_____
_____
_____
_____
_____
_____
_____
_____
_____
_____
_____
_____
_____
_____
_____
_____
_____
_____
_____
_____
_____
_____
_____
_____
_____
_____
_____
_____

23

Queen Goddess, ruler of you, tell me how you envision your life without fear, drama and a backward view of that brick wall.

24

Write down those stories you hold near and dear. You know the ones that have a hold over you. (For today's entry, I recommend using a separate notebook so you can tear the pages out.)

When you are done, follow the guide in chapter four of *The Goddess You* and perform a clearing or fire ceremony to release them.

Principle Seven

Chakra Basics

Chakra points are our passageways to going deeper within and connecting to the soul self at a higher vibration. Clearing these points with meditation and energy work brings forth another level of healing. Each chakra point in your body is a pathway for energy to enter and bring you into closer connection with God or your higher power.

The seven main chakra points are:

7th chakra **Crown**
Located at the crown of the head.

6th chakra **Third Eye**
Located in the center of the forehead.

5th chakra **Throat**
Located in the center of the neck or throat area.

4th chakra **Heart**
Located in the center of the chest.

3rd chakra **Solar Plexus**
Located at the bottom of the rib cage.

2nd chakra **Sacral**
Located at the bellybutton.

1st chakra **Root**
Located at the base of the spine or pelvic area.

Read more about the chakra system in
The Goddess You.

I recommend that you do the Chakra meditation in chapter seven of *The Goddess You* before each of the next four journal entries.

25

Today is all about the **root** chakra. Use the breath work to bring your attention to your **root** chakra and spend time being in that energy. Write down all your findings, feelings and sensations. You know what I mean—"Nancy Drew it."

26

Today you can move into the **sacral**, then **solar plexus** area. Spend time on each one and write down all your impressions.

27

Today we move up to the **heart** and **throat** chakras. Be sure to take plenty of time for each one, and give me all the details!

28

Third eye and **crown** are your chakra focus today. Don't rush through this. You have come so far—give it your all! Pour out all your findings right here with your magic pen!

Principle
Eight

Healthy, Wealthy and Wise

Knowing your body's energy or vibrational rate helps you know just what your body, mind and soul need to maintain your highest, healthiest vibrational energy level. Since you know everything is made up of energy, it's time to take that knowledge to the next level by introducing you to how to live healthy, wealthy and wise for your personal well-being.

You vibrate to your own unique energetic rate, which means you will need specific things to keep your energy healthy and running smoothly. The next journal entries will help you see what serves your highest and best good, as well as what is no longer serving you. Get ready—this is the fun stuff!

A healthy vibrational you comes from eating foods that serve your highest and best good. Make a list of your daily food intake for the next four journal entries. Before eating, I want you to feel that food's vibration. Start by holding the food in your hand while closing your eyes. Jot down your findings.

Bonus: Journal how food matters to your well-being.

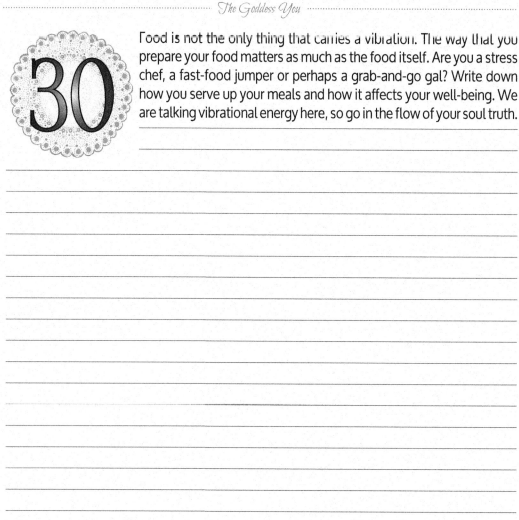

30 Food is not the only thing that carries a vibration. The way that you prepare your food matters as much as the food itself. Are you a stress chef, a fast-food jumper or perhaps a grab-and-go gal? Write down how you serve up your meals and how it affects your well-being. We are talking vibrational energy here, so go in the flow of your soul truth.

31

Wealth is not just money, honey. Wealth is how you welcome in new energy including money. Tell me how the money that flows in your life affects your energy.

Oh and P.S.—if you say there is no flow, you may need to clear up some energy to make room.... just sayin'.

32

A wise man once said, "Ask and you will receive, and your joy will be complete" (John 16:24). Jesus invites us to ask for what we need, as we shall receive the Lord's blessings in return. Go on now, ask...

Principle
Nine

Keep Calm and Carry the Flock on

Entering your crazy stress state is never a good feeling. The aftermath of crazy energy is crappy—not only for you, but for others as well. Finding your calm in the challenging times is important for the well-being of your mind, body and soul. By finding your strength in the moment of crazy and bringing your Zen back into focus, you will train your brain to stay in forward love-thinking and shift Shmego's fear-talk out of the way.

Remember, the power of breathing in through your nose and out through your mouth immediately brings your focus forward. Practice the breath technique in new places like the bank or grocery store. This will help you to learn how to ignore your surroundings while you get centered. No one needs to know what you are doing. Walk and balance, breathe, shop and balance, breathe, travel and balance, breathe! Ahhhh ... that feels so good, right?

33

Let's talk about your freak state and tell me all about how you look, feel and act when you're in that crazy zone.

34

Let's chat about compassion without compromise. How can you implement that energy into your life?

_____
_____
_____
_____
_____
_____
_____
_____
_____
_____
_____
_____
_____
_____
_____
_____
_____
_____
_____
_____
_____
_____
_____
_____
_____
_____
_____
_____
_____
_____
_____
_____
_____
_____
_____
_____
_____
_____
_____
_____

35

Layering the energy from the previous lessons into this very moment, try a meditative breath exercise while reflecting on the energy that calm has to offer you—and "Nancy Drew it"! Write down all your detective details here.

36

Releasing your feelings is the best way to allow the energy to flow out of you. There are high vibrational ways to release your energy without freakin' out—so what are they?

_____

_____

_____

_____

_____

_____

_____

_____

_____

_____

_____

_____

_____

_____

_____

_____

_____

_____

_____

_____

_____

_____

_____

_____

_____

_____

_____

_____

_____

_____

_____

_____

_____

_____

_____

_____

Principle
Ten

Help I've Lost My Balance and I Can't Get Up

Your balance comes from layering the 12 principles together, but let's get real—you're human and you're bound to lose your balance once in awhile. And when you can't seem to find the strength on your own to get back to your Zen, you can place the call for backup help to remind you that you've got this. A prayer of petition, a trusted friend, a spouse, a loved one or a God-based energy healer are just some of the ways you can reach out to get help when you need it. Knowing how to get back in balance is your newfound survival tool.

37

Tell me about when you loose your balance—what it looks like and feels like. Then tell me how you can change and shift into calm by using *The Goddess You* principles.

Meditation is your friend. How are you engaging your meditation, friend? Are you finding time each day to be with the quiet, reflective, peaceful, beautiful, meditative you? Take a few moments to get to that sweet space within your breath. Then write down the feelings and findings you've discovered in your meditative self.

39

Faith is needed to maintain healthy balance in your life. Let's chat about what faith means to you and how faith supports you.

_____
_____
_____
_____
_____
_____
_____
_____
_____
_____
_____
_____
_____
_____
_____
_____
_____
_____
_____
_____
_____
_____
_____
_____
_____
_____
_____
_____
_____
_____
_____
_____
_____
_____

40

Balancing Your Energy 101: You're the teacher now. Lead the way with your new lesson plan on the lines below.

Principle
Eleven

Mind, Body, Spirit

Living in alignment with your soul self comes from implementing all *The Goddess You* principles simultaneously. The mind, body and spirit working as one high-vibrational being open you to that a-ha moment you've been working toward. Try the energy scale to see if you are living in alignment. If 1 is the lowest and 10 is the highest, where is your vibrational rate on the energy scale? From now until the end of the journal, take note of your vibrational rate daily.

41

Meditation with intent and prayer opens the many Inner doorways to God. Sit in meditation with the intent and prayer to open your inner connection with the Beloved. Invite the loving energy to flow through the core of your being. Share all the details of your experience!

Reflecting over the past 41 entries, how are you feeling and what energy has shifted in your life? Are you setting your daily intent? Are you living in your highest vibration?

✿ Bonus I encourage you to review each of *The Goddess You* principles and journal entries you have made thus far, taking time if need be to re-do any one that feels like it is not completely aligning with you. You may find that you need a bit more time to open up to the energy of a principle before you continue on with confidence.

Write down your review findings:

_____
_____
_____
_____
_____
_____
_____
_____
_____
_____
_____
_____
_____
_____
_____
_____
_____
_____
_____
_____
_____
_____
_____
_____
_____
_____
_____
_____
_____
_____

43

Let's chat about your chakras. Tell me how your energy flows and how healthy you feel it is. Is it time for a clearing, or maybe it is time to make an appointment with a (God-based) energy healer?

44

What Is the tone In which your Inner Goddess speaks to you? Describe her in full detail.

Principle
Twelve

Intuitive Gifted You

Rockin' out your Goddess You requires your intuitive connection to be steadfast and strong. Faith in God and in yourself is a proven tool to achieve your soul alignment. Follow the "Knowing Your Gifts" guided meditation in *The Goddess You* and journal your experience.

45

Opening your intuition requires faith in your inner guidance system. Tell me how you are listening to your inner guidance— your beautiful, intuitive self.

46

Gifts are how God's energy flows through us, while talents are how we express the Divine energy. You are unique in your talents and gifts. List talents you have and then list the gift— the aspect you use to help those talents flow.

_____

_____

_____

_____

_____

_____

_____

_____

_____

_____

_____

_____

_____

_____

_____

_____

_____

_____

_____

_____

_____

_____

_____

_____

_____

_____

_____

_____

_____

_____

_____

_____

_____

_____

_____

_____

_____

_____

_____

_____

_____

47

Intuition, grooving side-by-side with your gifts and talents, is just... awesome, lovely and powerful. Tell me your thoughts and feelings on this statement.

_____
_____
_____
_____
_____
_____
_____
_____
_____
_____
_____
_____
_____
_____
_____
_____
_____
_____
_____
_____
_____
_____
_____
_____
_____
_____
_____
_____
_____
_____
_____
_____
_____
_____
_____
_____
_____
_____

48

Describe who you are in this very moment.

_____
_____
_____
_____
_____
_____
_____
_____
_____
_____
_____
_____
_____
_____
_____
_____
_____
_____
_____
_____
_____
_____
_____
_____
_____
_____
_____
_____
_____
_____
_____
_____
_____
_____
_____
_____
_____
_____
_____
_____

❀ *Bonus*

Sharing your gifts with others opens your compassion for all. Tell me how you are being of service.

❃ Bonus

Being in soul alignment allows you to know your soul path and soul work. This is the moment to let it all out. What is your soul purpose?

YAHOO, you did it! Great job!

You just finished *The Goddess You* journal experience. How do you feel? Remember you can come back to the journal anytime, moving through the different prompts to deepen your connection to your soul self.

Rock on you Bad-Ass Goddess Gal!

Blessings,

xx Jeanne

_____

Date of completion

Ready to social share follow the links

       tweetables   #Badassgoddessgal
                                  #thegoddessyou

About the Author

Author, Jeanne Street is a dynamic woman. To list her many contributions and accomplishments would be an insult to her humble nature.

Wherever there is a need, Street finds a way to lend a helping hand. Her life embodies the essence of service, compassion, gratitude and love.

She is a family first kind of woman. Devoted to her husband and soul mate of 31 years, together they are the proud parents of four grown children and grandparents to 3 and counting.

If you are lucky enough to find yourself in her inner circle, which grows daily, you will find yourself enriched by her love and generosity. But Street does not stop with close friends and family. Her gifts are many and she longs to help as many souls as possible.

Street is a gifted spiritual medium and healer. Admittedly she has always known of these gifts, although she had not fully understood and embraced them until recent years. As she began to trust spirit's messages, they became a clear truth that she could no longer keep within.

Through her classes and client healing sessions Street is now able to witness the profound manifestation of energy shift and divine connection that her clients display. That was the catalyst for writing this book, because "when Spirit speaks, Street listens."

It has always been her deepest desire to guide others to heal themselves. Street is honored to share what has been gifted to her through her connection with Spirit in her book, *The Goddess You* principles for living In soul alignment as well as the books companion The Goddess You Journal.

You can now find Jeanne Street leading her classes and providing her healing work at her Inspirit Healing Studio at 346 Main Street, Woodbury, CT

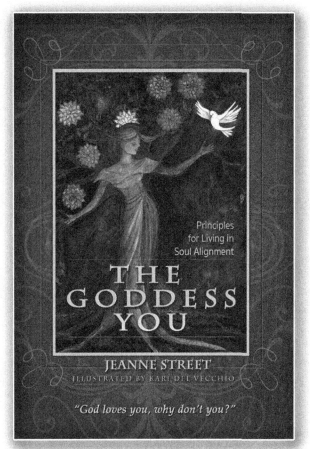

Don't go it alone...

Messages from Spirit guide, lift and aide you on your personal journey

LET'S CONNECT

This journal is just the beginning of a larger conversation. I would love it if you would visit me on the web or reach out on social media.
Start at **www.jeannestreet.com** or find me on social media.

Email   jeanne@jeannestreet.com
Face Book   www.facebook.com/JeanneStreetReikiMaster
Twitter   @jeannehealer
Instagram   www.instagram.com/jeannestreetmedium
Pinterest   www.pinterest.com/jeannestreet
YouTube   www.youtube.com/channel/jeannestreet
Website   jeannestreet.com

#THEGODDESSYOU

CPSIA information can be obtained
at www.ICGtesting.com
Printed in the USA
BVOW04*0443200817
491807BV00011B/6/P